Hello!
I am a bear.

I0108770

Bears are mammals, just like humans.

That means they have fur and give birth to live babies.

Bears have a great sense of smell. It helps them find food.

Bears have excellent hearing and can detect sounds from far away.

Most bears are "omnivorous".

That means I eat both plants and meat.

Yummy... Bamboo for dinner again!

However, pandas are herbivores which means they mostly eat plants.

Bears have a diverse diet.

Depending on the species, bears can eat fish, insects, and small mammals.

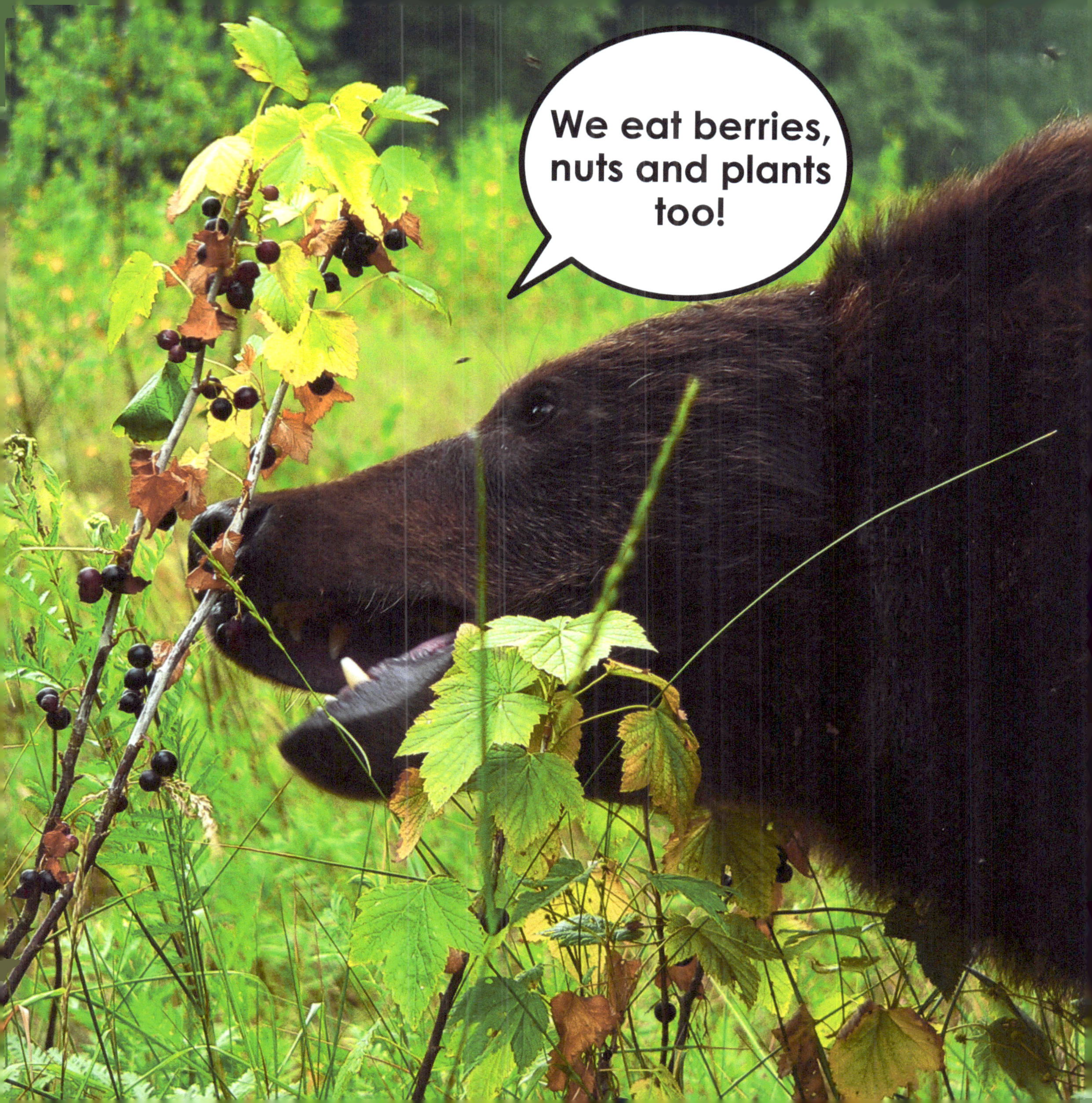
We eat berries, nuts and plants too!

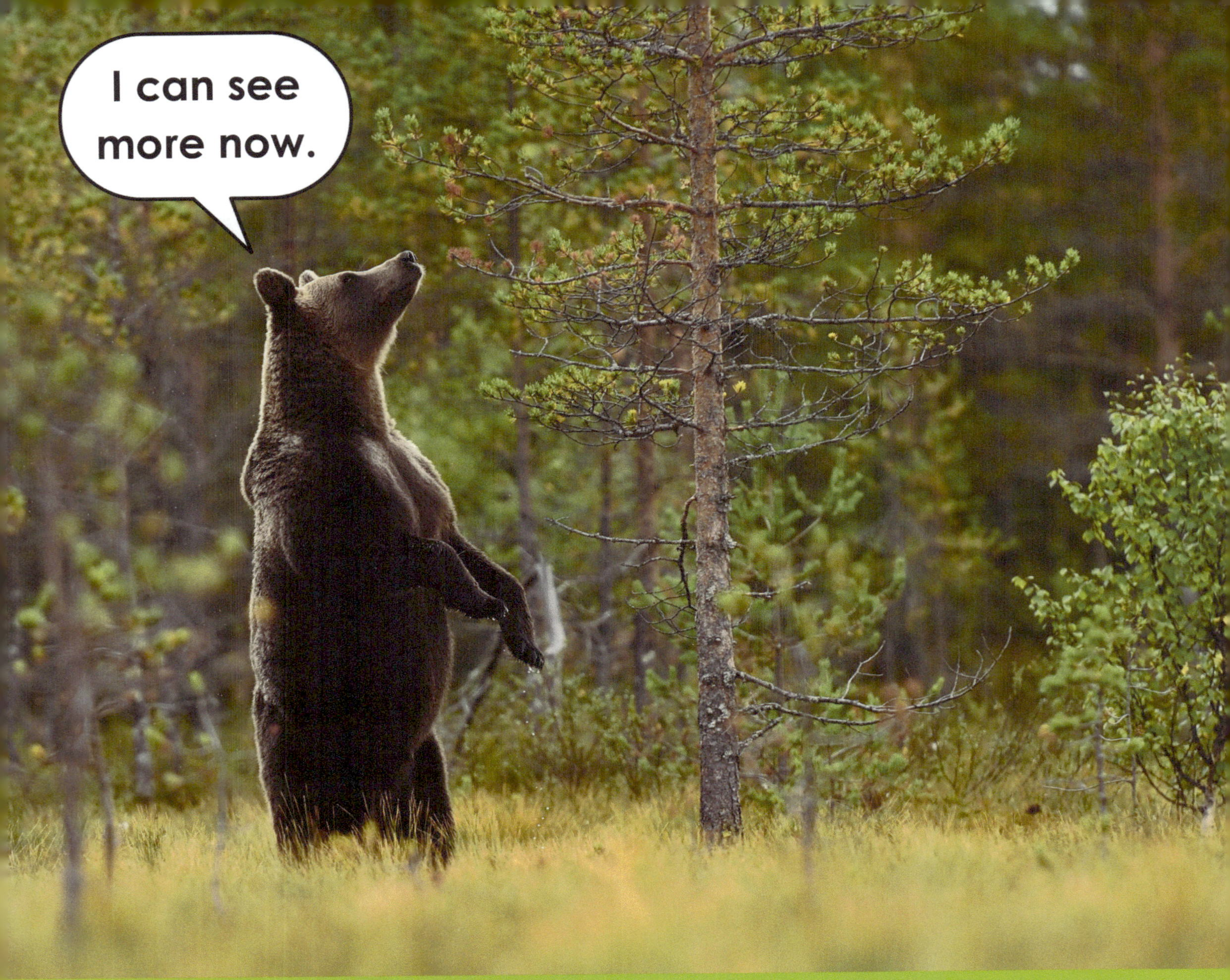

Bears can stand on
their hind legs.

This allows bears to see better and reach food on higher branches.

Bears hibernate during winter.

Goodnight.

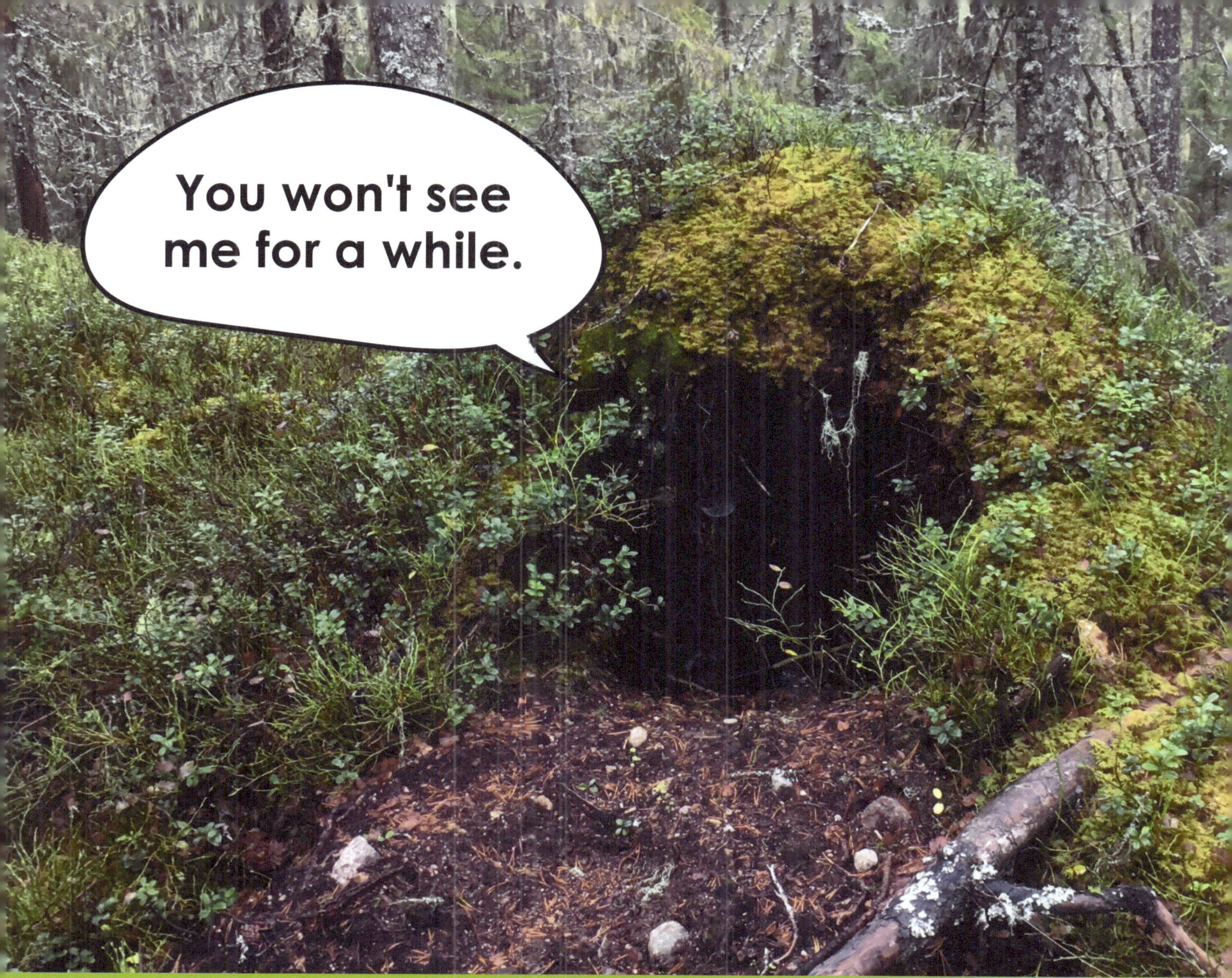

Bears find a den, curl up, and sleep until spring.

Bears can protect each other and help one another find food.

A group of bears is called a "sleuth" or a "sloth".

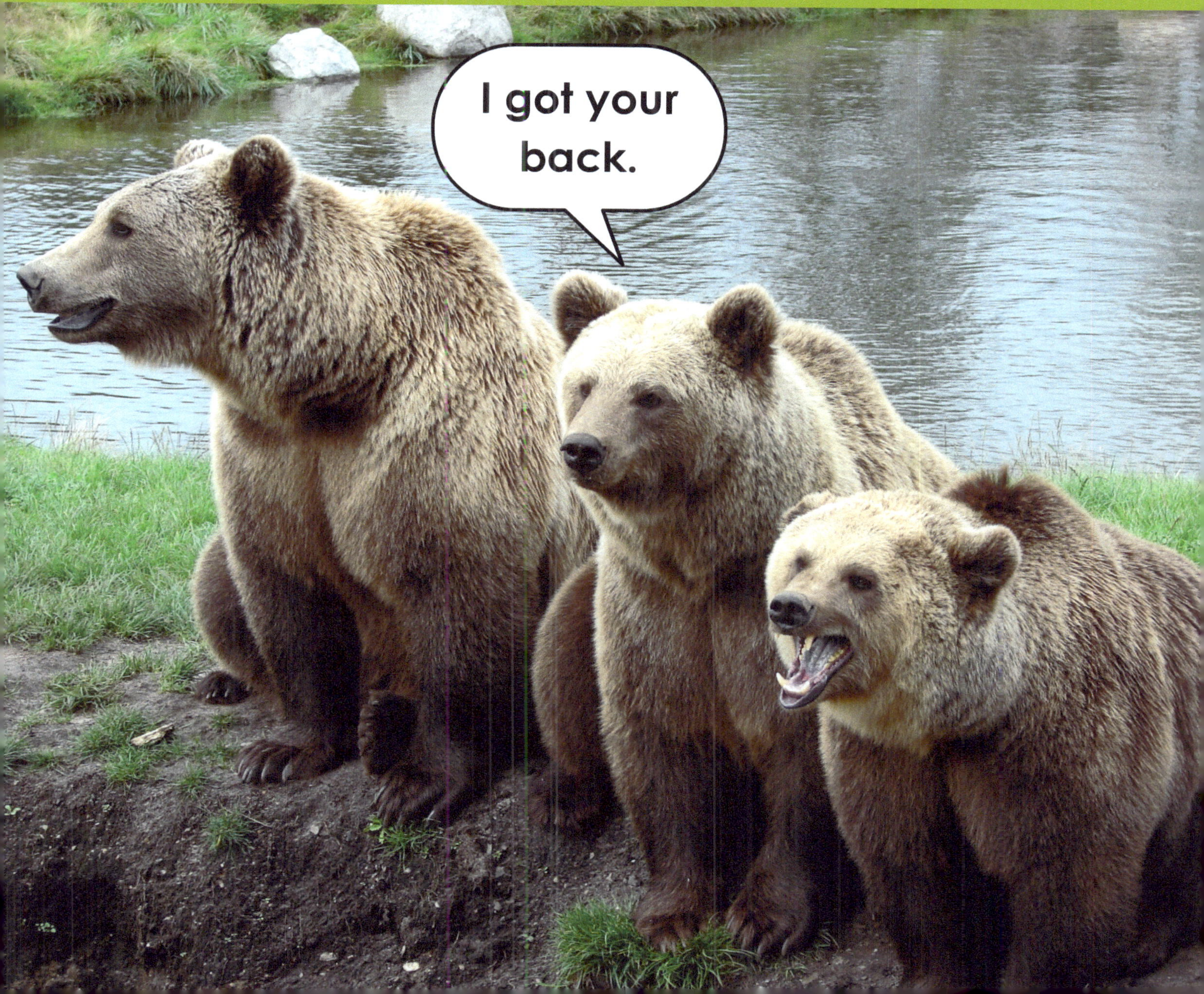

Cubs are baby bears, and they are born very small and helpless.

You've got a lot to learn from me!

Cubs stay with their mothers until they are around two years old, learning survival skills.

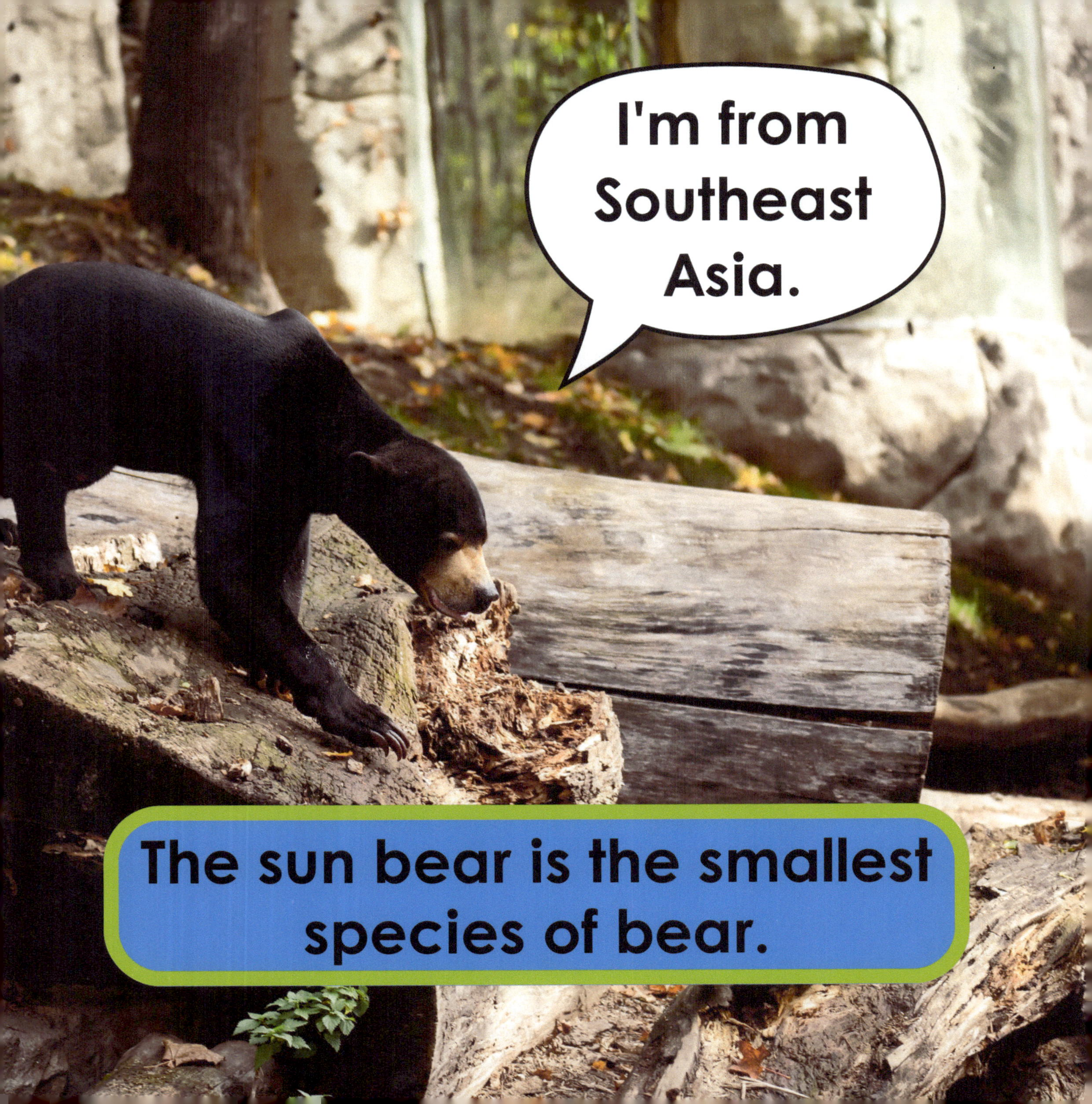

The sun bear is the smallest species of bear.

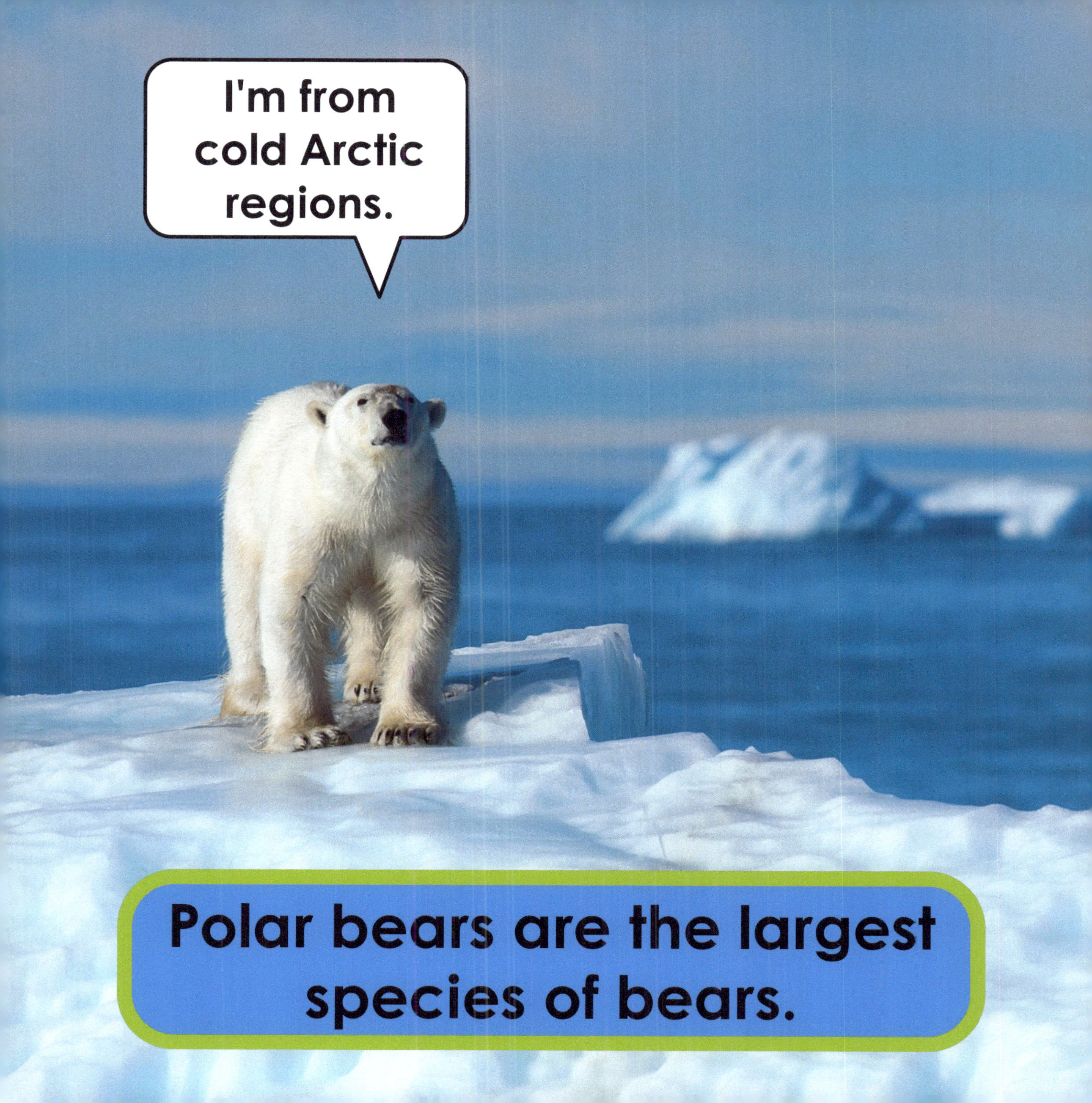

Polar bears are the largest species of bears.

Some bears can run up to 40 miles (64km) per hour.

Bears have sharp claws that help them catch food and climb trees.

Bears have a thick layer of fat called blubber, which helps keep them warm in cold weather.

Bears have a layer of fur called guard hairs, which helps protect their skin from scratches and insects.

Bears love to swim and are excellent swimmers.

We are endurance swimmers!

Some bears, like polar bears, can swim long distances in search of food.

Bears have a unique way of marking their territory.

Who else has been here?

They rub their bodies on trees and leave a scent.

Bears also use their claws to leave scratch marks so other bears know it's their area.

Bears are intelligent animals.

Bears have a great memory and can remember places where they found food or encountered danger.

I don't need a map.

There are eight different species of bears: the polar bear, brown bear, black bear, panda bear, sloth bear, sun bear, spectacled bear, and the giant panda.

Bears are found in different parts of the world...

Where are you from?

...including North America, South America, Europe, and Asia.

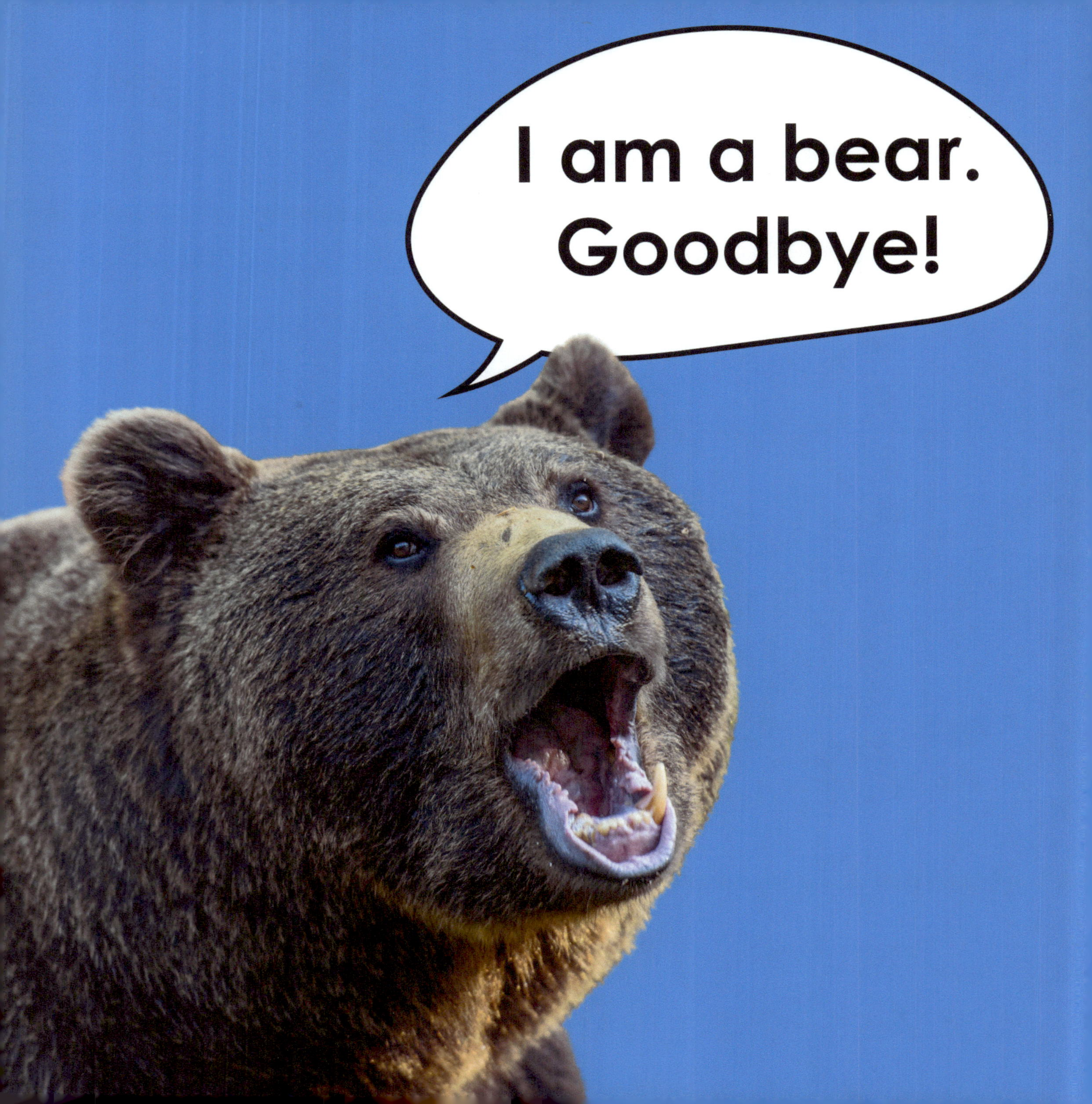
I am a bear.
Goodbye!

Want more?

COLLECT THEM ALL!

... and more

ActiveBrainsBooks.com

Hello parents!

scan here

Visit us to find out about new releases and **FREE** offers. We'll let you know when we have a new release coming out and how you can get it for FREE.

And you can cast your vote for what book we make next!

or visit here

ActiveBrainsBooks.com

---

scan here

Let us know what you think. As an independent publisher, your honest reviews mean a lot to us and our business. We'd love to hear from you!

amazon.com/review/create-review/

or visit here

FOLLOW US on Amazon.

amazon.com/author/activebrainsbooks

ACTIVE BRAINS

ActiveBrainsBooks.com

www.ingramcontent.com/pod-product-compliance
Lightning Source LLC
Chambersburg PA
CBHW042056040426
42447CB00003B/248